ALL ABOUT ANIMALS IN THE SEA

All About Giant Octopuses

Kerrily Sapet

EZ READERS
AN IMPRINT OF MITCHELL LANE PUBLISHERS

CREATING YOUNG NONFICTION READERS

EZ Readers offer nonfiction for beginning readers in PreK through first grade, using simple language, clear illustrations, and engaging facts to build vocabulary and confidence.

TIPS FOR READING NONFICTION WITH BEGINNING READERS

Talk about Nonfiction

Begin by explaining that nonfiction books give us information that is true. The book will be organized around a specific topic or idea, and we may learn new facts through reading.

Look at the Parts

Most nonfiction books have helpful features. Our *EZ Readers* include color photographs and graphic aids, a table of contents, a glossary, and an index. Share the purpose of these features with your reader.

Color Photos and Graphic Aids

A lot of information can be found by "reading" photos, charts, maps, and other graphic aids found within nonfiction texts. Help your reader learn more about the different ways information can be displayed.

Table of Contents

Located at the front of the book, this list shows the big ideas within the text and the page numbers where they can be found.

Glossary

Located at the back of the book, the glossary defines key words and phrases that are related to the topic. These words and phrases can be found in the text in colored type.

Index

Located at the back of the book, an index is an alphabetical list of topics and the page numbers where they can be found.

With a little help and guidance about reading nonfiction, you can feel good about introducing a young reader to the world of *EZ Readers* nonfiction books.

EZ Readers is an imprint of:

Mitchell Lane PUBLISHERS

2001 SW 31st Avenue
Hallandale, FL 33009
mitchelllanepub.com

First Edition, 2026.

Author: Kerrily Sapet
Editor: Morgan Brody

ISBN 979-8-89260-838-1(library binding)
ISBN 979-8-90145-037-6 (paperback)
ISBN 979-8-89260-940-1 (ebook)

LC record available at https://lccn.loc.gov/2025950870

Photo credits: Shutterstock, ROMAN RYBALKO cover, 1; Shutterstock, Northern Owl cover, 1, 2, 3, 4, 8, 15, 19; Shutterstock, ChristopherRM, cover, 1; Shutterstock, Pong471, cover, 1; Adobe, 3, 13, 14; Shutterstock, Irina WS, 5; Shutterstock, pr2is, 6–7; Shutterstock, Olga Visavi, 9; Shutterstock, Kondratuk Aleksei, 10–11; Shutterstock, Vittorio Bruno, 12–13, 22; Shutterstock, Martin Voeller 14, 22; Wikimedia Commons, Un-chan, 18 Wikimedia Commons, Erin McKittrick, 18 Shutterstock, Konstantin Novikov, 20, 21; Wikimedia Commons, Comingio Merculiano (1845-1915) in Jatta Giuseppe (1860-1903), 21, 22; Wikimedia Commons, NOAA, 22; Wikimedia Commons, sthee2010, 22; Shutterstock, Jesus Cobaleda, 22; Shutterstock, Samuel Borges Photography, 22

Table of Contents

Meeting An Ocean Wonder

Imagine you are in a boat.
The water is cold and clear.
You float over rocks.

You see a reddish-pink animal swimming below. Its eight arms tap and grip the rocks. A giant octopus! Each arm is as long as your bed. It weighs as much as a large dog.

Octopus Watching

The octopus has a soft body and big eyes. The sticky **suction** cups on its arms can touch, taste, and smell. Picture having noses and tongues on your arms! Each arm has 280 suction cups—from quarter-sized to the size of this "o."

OCTOPUS OBSERVATION!

Octopuses do not have bones.

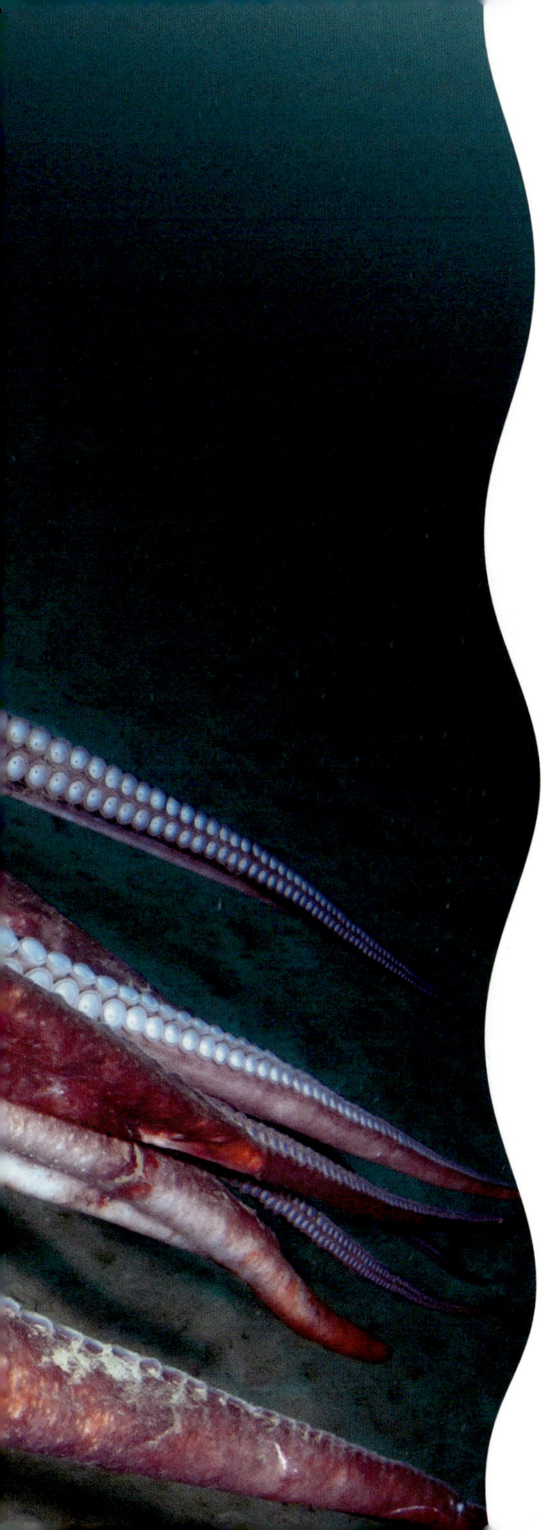

You peek over the side of the boat. The octopus swims. It sucks in water. It pushes the water out through a tube called a **siphon**. When the water shoots out, the octopus zooms the other way—like a balloon when you let go.

You see one octopus. Giant octopuses live alone. The octopus changes color. It matches the rocks. Octopuses turn colors to hide and show their feelings. They also squirt **ink** to hide.

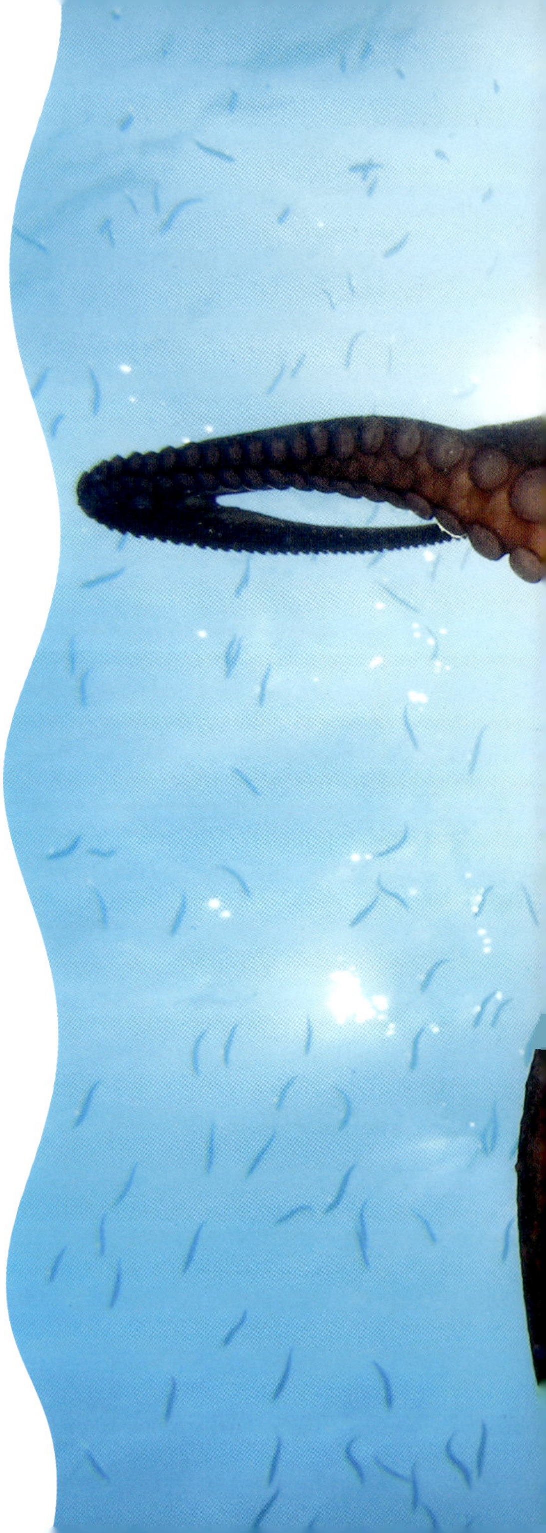

OCTOPUS OBSERVATION!

Excited octopuses turn red.

OCTOPUS OBSERVATION!

Octopuses build doors for their dens.

Looking for Food

Fish swim past. The octopus is not eating. Octopuses **hunt** at night. They eat clams and fish. Octopuses have hard, sharp beaks to bite their food. They eat in their **dens**.

Octopuses are smart. They open jars to get food. They solve mazes. Octopuses remember people.

Where Do Giant Octopuses Live?

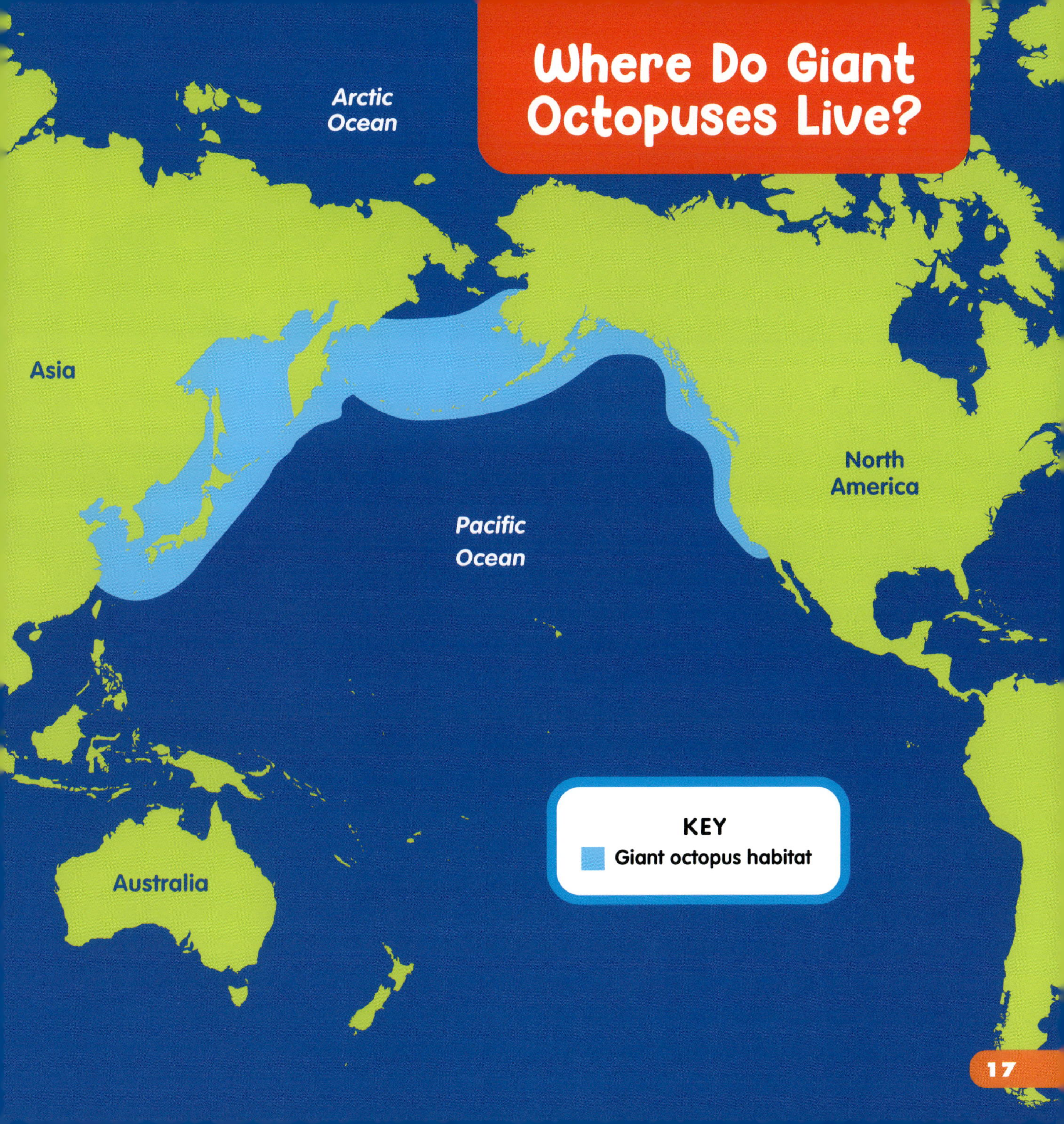

OCTOPUS OBSERVATION!

Octopuses are born with 14 tiny suction cups on each arm.

Octopus Families and the Future

A mother octopus lays many eggs. She keeps them safe. When the babies **hatch**, they are the size of a pea. They float and eat bits of food.

Giant octopuses can live five years. Sharks and people eat them. **Pollution** harms them. Someday you might see a real giant octopus!

Parts of a Giant Octopus

Arm
One of eight long parts an octopus uses to move and feel its world.

Beak
The hard mouth an octopus uses to bite and eat food.

Mantle
The soft bag on an octopus's body that holds its three hearts and stomach.

Siphon
The tube octopuses use to swim and squirt ink.

Suction cups
Sticky round parts on an octopus's arms that help it taste, smell, and grip objects.

Glossary

den (den)
a home where animals live

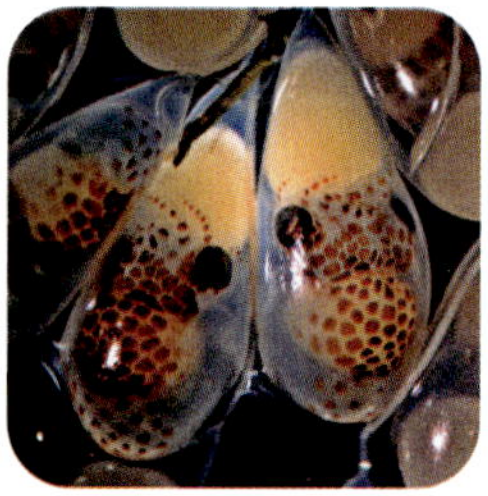

hatch (hach)
to come out of an egg

hunt (huhnt)
to chase another animal for food

ink (ING-k)
dark liquid an octopus spits into the water to hide

pollution (PO-loo-shun)
dirty air, water, or land

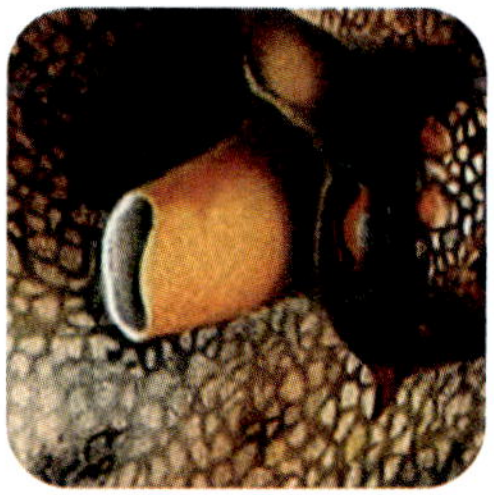

siphon (SI-fun)
a tube that helps water move from one place to another

suction (SUK-shun)
when something sucks an object in, like when you use a straw to drink water

Quiz

1. Do octopuses have bones?

   A. Yes B. No

2. Are octopuses smart?

   A. Yes B. No

3. Do octopuses eat sharks?

   A. Yes B. No

4. Can octopuses change color?

   A. Yes B. No

ANSWER KEY:

1. No
2. Yes
3. No
4. Yes

Further Reading

Clarke, Ginjer. *Octopus!: Smartest in the Sea?* New York, NY: Penguin Young Readers, 2024.

Spencer, Erin. *The Incredible Octopus.* North Adams, MA: Storey Publishing, 2024.

Towler, Paige. *Mysterious, Marvelous Octopus!* Washington, D.C.: National Geographic Kids, 2024.

On the Internet

Animals A to Z
https://www.montereybayaquarium.org/animals/animals-a-to-z/giant-pacific-octopus
Learn about the octopus at the aquarium.

Octopuses Facts for Kids
https://kids.nationalgeographic.com/animals/invertebrates/facts/octopus
Read more and watch a video about giant octopuses.

Eight Strange and Wonderful Facts About Octopuses
https://www.sheddaquarium.org/stories/eight-strange-and-wonderful-facts-about-octopuses
See pictures and watch an octopus swimming and solving a puzzle.

Index

About the Author

Kerrily Sapet has written more than 30 books for kids. She lives near Chicago with her family. Sapet once watched an octopus eating at the Monterrey Aquarium. She likes visiting the octopus at the Shedd Aquarium. When it's not hiding, it crawls around the tank. She loves to read about octopuses. Sapet has never seen an octopus in the ocean. She hopes to see one someday.